100 PROMPTS
for ROMANCE WRITERS

ANNETTE ELTON

100 PROMPTS

for ROMANCE WRITERS

ANNETTE ELTON

STERLING
New York

STERLING
New York

An Imprint of Sterling Publishing
387 Park Avenue South
New York, NY 10016

© 2014 by Annette Brownlee Elton

ISBN 978-1-4549-1424-2

Distributed in Canada by Sterling Publishing
c/o Canadian Manda Group, 165 Dufferin Street
Toronto, Ontario, Canada M6K 3H6
Distributed in the United Kingdom by GMC Distribution Services
Castle Place, 166 High Street, Lewes, East Sussex, England BN7 1XU
Distributed in Australia by Capricorn Link (Australia) Pty. Ltd.
P.O. Box 704, Windsor, NSW 2756, Australia

For information about custom editions, special sales, and premium
and corporate purchases, please contact Sterling Special Sales at
800-805-5489 or specialsales@sterlingpublishing.com.

Manufactured in the United States of America

2 4 6 8 10 9 7 5 3 1

www.sterlingpublishing.com

CONTENTS

INTRODUCTION

Year after year Romance fiction outsells every other fiction genre. According to Romance Writers of America, romance books sold an estimated $1.35 billion in 2013, and there's no sign of the genre slowing down.

With the growing trend of self-published authors becoming mainstream successes, the sky's the limit. Self-published authors such as Bella Andre can sell millions of books; last year that phenomenal success led Andre to a lucrative book deal with Harlequin MIRA. And as of this writing self-published erotic romance author E. L. James has sold more than 100 million copies of her record-breaking *Fifty Shades* trilogy globally and has gone on to become one of the highest-earning authors ever.

With a great story idea you too could have a best seller on your hands. So what is a great story? There are two basic elements that are fundamental to every beloved romantic novel, from *Twilight* by Stephenie Meyer to *Outlander* by Diana Gabaldon: a central love story and a satisfying ending. What happens in your story, how your lovers find their way to one another, and how it ends, is all up to you.

The key to a great romance novel isn't beautifully written prose or snappy dialogue—though they can add interest. The best-selling and most enjoyable books all tell great stories. And a great story can be difficult to create without a spark of a story capturing your attention and setting your imagination afire.

Romance writing prompts are different than the traditional writing prompt. Rather than striving to create a scene, they're designed to help you imagine and create a best-selling romance novel. Romantic scenarios are presented and questions are asked to help guide you forward as you create fully realized story lines.

This journal is divided into the most widely beloved and recognized romance genres of our time. There's something for everyone, including the widely popular paranormal romance genre, inspirational fiction, erotic romance, and even some young adult prompts. Of course, you can bend any one of these writing prompts to your will and mold it to a genre that best suits you. There's no reason why a prompt that's categorized as a paranormal romance couldn't be modified to be a historical romance, or vice versa, and heroines can become heroes as your story line takes shape.

START WRITING

Make your way through the prompts by writing a little each day, or find an idea that inspires you and focus solely on that idea.

Use the prompts to get you through a writer's block or to launch your newest romance novel. There are no rules here—shape each writing prompt to fit your needs and goals. ◼

CONTEMPORARY

Humorous,
Urban, Chick Lit

NO. 1

Your heroine has a checklist of her perfect man. She made the list when she was sixteen years old and just recently uncovered it. Laughing at her criteria back then, she and her friends set out to find a man that fits her teenage standards. They find him.

Who is he, and what happens? What's on a sixteen-year-old's "perfect man" checklist?

NO. 2

Your heroine is sitting alone at a trendy bar waiting for her blind date to show up, someone she only exchanged e-mails with online. She is a little jaded as these dates usually turn out to be frogs rather than princes. Someone who vaguely resembles the blurry picture from her date's profile taps her on the shoulder—she almost faints when she sees him.

Why is she so shocked? Was he gorgeous? Does she know him? How does their date end?

NO. 3

Your heroine is boarding a New York-to-London redeye for business; she has an important presentation the next day. She takes her window seat and settles in, hoping to have the row to herself so she can stretch out and sleep. However just before the airplane door closes, a handsome man dashes down the aisle, bound for the window seat next to hers.

Who is the man? A stranger or her lover? What happens between them during the flight?

NO. 4

Your heroine is a successful, driven defense attorney. She is about to start work on a high-profile trial, but once again she's going up against a particular prosecutor who has it in for her—but he also has a hold on her heart.

What is their history? What happens between them during the trial?

NO. 5

Your heroine is thrown under the bus by a coworker and given the lead of a tanking campaign/division. She feels like she's been set up to fail . . . even worse, she has a huge crush on her boss and now she's going to look like an idiot and probably get fired.

What has she just been put in charge of, and why is it failing? What does she do? How does the boss react to her success/failure?

NO. 6

Your heroine is a professional date planner. People pay her to plan and organize extravagant, romantic dates. Her own love life sucks, but she's great at what she does. An angry client shows up at her office. His girlfriend broke up with him on their date. He was going to propose.

What happens next?

NO. 7

Your heroine needs to get married and convinces her gay friend to help her out. All is going according to plan until she meets her fiancé's brother. Everything starts unraveling.

Why does she need to get married? Why does her friend agree to help her, and what happens when the wedding plans begin unraveling?

Your heroine is headed to the local jail to bail out a family member. She's surprised by what happened and who was involved. Even more surprised is the cop who is there to help her with the paperwork.

Who is he? How do they know each other? Why is she at the jail to bail someone out? Who is it, and what happened to put them there?

Your heroine is a food blogger, and her travels have taken her to some of the strangest destinations in the world. None is stranger than the one she is visiting today. She gets out of the car and is surrounded by anxious and excited faces. They've been eagerly anticipating her arrival. Through the crowd she spots one face she never thought she'd see again.

Who is he? Where are they? How did he end up in this unique location? What do they do next?

NO. 10

Your heroine is recovering from being dumped by her boyfriend. His estranged wife of several years has returned and wants to patch things up. The fact that your heroine and her ex work together is making things difficult, but they're about to get worse when she discovers she's pregnant.

What does she do?

NO. 11

Your heroine has agreed to be a surrogate. She runs into a man she had a one-night stand with a few months ago, and he mistakenly assumes the child is his.

For who and why has she decided to be a surrogate? Why does the man assume he's the father? Why did your heroine have a one-night stand? What happens?

NO. 12

Your heroine has no family left. Her beloved but estranged younger brother has just died, and the only connection she has to him is his newborn daughter. Desperate for a connection to this baby, your heroine visits her sister-in-law (without telling her they are related) to apply for the job of nanny. She gets the job. The young mother and her new child are under the care of the mother's attractive and widowed father.

What happens when he discovers your heroine's connection to his grandchild?

NO.
13

Your hero is dealing with PTSD, post-traumatic stress disorder. He falls into the arms of your heroine and for a short time, one night perhaps, he feels like she can save him. Then he has a panic attack and decides it's best if he leaves. A year or so later he runs into her at a family reunion, and she's on the arm of his brother.

What happens?

No. 14

Your heroine was jilted at the altar when her fiancé announced that he loves her sister instead. Humiliated and angry more than hurt, she devises a plan with a man her sister loves dearly. The goal is to make her ex jealous, but it backfires when the two can't keep their hands off of each other.

What happens? Why does your hero agree to be a pawn?

PARANORMAL

Fantasy,
Supernatural,
Time Travel

NO. 15

Your heroine has lost her fiancé/husband. She goes to a medium to try to reach out to him on the "other side." During the session, however, the medium is unable to contact him. Instead, a deceased family member steps forward and tells the medium that your heroine's spouse/fiancé isn't on the "other side" . . . because he isn't dead.

What does your heroine do? Is he really dead, or is he alive? Who is your hero? For example, it could be the presumed dead spouse, or it could be the man who helps your heroine pull herself together when she gets false hope that her loved one is alive.

Your heroine suddenly finds herself bouncing around in time. One day she's in the 1920s, and the next she's in the 1980s. The only constant is a mystery man, whom she sees in every era.

Why is she bouncing around in time, and who is the man?

NO. 17

Your heroine, unlucky in love, learns that she can write a letter to her younger self and she'll receive it. The letter will be able to travel back in time and tell your heroine something that she needs to know to have a different, and presumably better, love life.

What does she write in the note? What happens? Does her younger self heed the message? How does the letter change her life?

Your hero is an artist, and he's been painting the same woman from his dreams for decades. Then she walks through the front door of his gallery.

What happens? What does he say to her? Who is she? Why has your hero been painting her all his life, and what's their connection?

Your heroine is avoiding a situation and heads to the local amusement park where she rides her favorite childhood ride over and over again. On the tenth time through the ride a man is suddenly sitting beside her.

Who is he? What happens? What situation is she avoiding, and how does their encounter change things for her?

NO. 20

Your heroine is in a cemetery at night. She hears a man talking quietly. Grabbing her pepper spray, she stops walking. In the distance she sees a man kneeling on the ground in front of a tombstone. He leans down and gently places a garland of flowers on the stone. Your heroine's watch alarm goes off. It's midnight. She glances down at her watch to turn it off, and when she looks up, the man is gone, but the flowers are still there. Curiosity drives your heroine to return to the cemetery the next night.

What does she see? What happens? And why was your heroine in the cemetery at night in the first place?

NO. 21

Your heroine is a veterinarian. A stranger comes in just as she's closing up. The stranger has an animal with him that is not like any other animal your heroine has ever seen (maybe it's part human). It needs help.

What is the animal, and why does it need help? Who is your hero? Why does he have this creature?

Your heroine runs a bed and breakfast that's haunted. Each guest receives the experience that the house deems is necessary to point them in the right direction for their life. Some people need to be scared straight. One guest, a man who checked in for a two-night stay, needs extra guidance.

How does your heroine help him? Why does he need extra guidance, and how does the house change his life?

NO. 23

Your heroine is a witch with the powers of seduction, but she's forbidden to use her abilities on your hero. Before she can make a decision about what to do, your hero uses his own powers to control her. She is livid.

What does she do to retaliate? How do they find their way to each other?

No. 24

Your heroine is on a trip to Iceland with her friends. During a tour of an ice cave, she wanders off and finds a man who is perfectly preserved; based on his attire, he must have lived hundreds of years ago. She mutters something; the ice begins thawing around the man; and he awakens.

Who is he, and what happens next?

NO. 25

Your heroine is part of the royal family. Her lover is a slave. He's removed from the castle and sent to a facility where his primary purpose will be for reproduction. Her lover is destined to be her king, not a brood stud. Your heroine defies orders and takes off to rescue her lover.

What does she find when she gets to the facility, and what happens? How do they escape, and where do they go once they're finally free?

NO. 26

Your heroine is an empath and can read the thoughts and feelings of others. She uses the skill for her job. Most of the time she can turn it on and off at will, but one particular man seems to break down her barriers. She cannot control her powers when he's around.

What is her job, and who is the man that wreaks havoc on her abilities? Is he doing it intentionally? Does he know what she does for a living? What happens?

Your villain is a dark and twisted sorceress who was spurned by a man. She learns that your heroine is being wooed by this same man. To have a little fun, your villain kidnaps the man and seals him in a vault.

What happens? What does your heroine do to save him?

NO. 28

Your heroine has accidentally captured what she thinks is a UFO on her video camera. She shares the weird video on social media and is an instant celebrity. She even has a new boyfriend who just may be the perfect man. Life is going well until she's kidnapped and learns that her perfect boyfriend isn't who she thought he was.

Who kidnaps her, and why? Who is her boyfriend, and what happens? How does he win back her trust and help her?

No. 29

Your heroine has better luck with dogs than she does with men. She's just been dumped, again. On the way home from the supermarket with a bag of ice cream and bubble bath, a dog starts following her. He follows her home and just won't go away. She takes him in. The next morning the dog is gone, and a man has appeared in his place.

What does she do next? Where did he come from?

No. 30

Your heroine instantly recognizes a new ranch hand on her family ranch as a love from a past life. He doesn't recognize her. In fact, he seems repelled by her.

How does she get his attention, and why is he so put off by her? What does she do to convince the cowboy that they're destined to be together?

Your heroine wakes up naked and in bed with a man she's been forbidden to see. She doesn't remember any of it and has never, ever, had a one-night stand. She tries to figure out what he did to her without bringing attention to their "association." She starts having memories about things that never happened, or did they?

Has someone blocked her memory, and is your hero the key to unlocking it? Why is she forbidden to see him?

NO. 32

Your heroine can see into other people's dreams. She's not supposed to, but she enjoys the energy she gets from it. Men in particular provide her with an energy she just cannot resist. But someone is killing her favorite dreamers. When her dreamers start dying, there's one particular man she must protect.

Why are they dying? How does she protect him? Who's killing them, and why?

NO. 33

Your heroine is loathe to play babysitter to her sister's stepdaughter. Being born into an aristocratic vampire family, the teenager is entitled and nothing but trouble. Things go from tenuous to unbearable when your heroine wakes to find her step-niece taking a late-night drink from the neck of your heroine's human lover.

What happens? Is she taunting your heroine, and if so, why?

No. 34

Your heroine has managed to hide from her nemesis, a powerful warlock, for centuries. His second-in-command finds her, brazenly appearing in her bedroom window one night.

What happens? Why does she need to hide from the warlock, and why does he want her back? What does your hero do to protect her?

NO. 35

It's your heroine's birthday. She blows out the candle on her cupcake for one and makes a wish. She wishes for a night with your hero, but he doesn't know she exists.

What happens when he shows up on her porch twenty minutes after she makes her wish? Why is he there, and what happens? Does she get her wish?

NO. 36

Your heroine must participate in a mating ritual. She's been preparing for this event for years. It's part of her culture. The problem is she doesn't want to do it.

Why not? Why is she required to participate, and what is the ritual? Who does she meet that helps change her mind about the ritual?

Your heroine has been cursed, literally. She tracks down the one person who can lift the curse and set her free to explore and enjoy romantic love.

Who cursed her, and why? What steps does she have to take with him to break the curse?

ROMANTIC SUSPENSE

Mystery, Thriller,
Military

NO. 38

Your heroine's fiancé died during a failed military operation. She blames his best friend—the only man that was with him when he died. To uncover the truth, she gets close to him and discovers more than she bargained for in the process.

What happened? How did her fiancé die? How did your hero's actions impact the event? (For example, maybe the fiancé actually sabotaged the procedure or made a mistake, and your hero did what he could to make him look like he died with honor.)

NO. 39

Your hero broke it off with your heroine years ago to protect her, but her connection to him has her in the sights of a sociopath. She escapes the first time, but your hero knows she won't be so lucky when he strikes again.

Why is someone after her? What is the goal? What is your hero hiding?

NO. 40

Your heroine made her way across raging floodwaters to help an elderly person who lives alone. Now they're both trapped. Who comes to help them? What happens? (Perhaps a handsome neighbor comes to help. Maybe the hero is a National Guardsman who gets stuck with them as well, or who rescues your heroine en route to save the elderly neighbor, and they have to take refuge.)

NO. 41

Your heroine is a documentary filmmaker. She captures something on film that people are willing to kill for. She knows this and turns to your hero for help.

What does she capture, and how does your hero try to help her out of this situation? What happens to them?

100 PROMPTS FOR ROMANCE WRITERS

NO. 42

Your heroine is investigating something and stumbles upon a mind-control project being led by your hero, who is also an investigator for the government. At first, she suspects he's the ringleader, but when she gets caught and becomes an unwitting lab rat, he comes to her rescue.

Who is behind the mind-control project? Why? What is their goal? What is your heroine investigating that leads her to this project? What happens when she is caught and becomes a lab rat?

NO. 43

Your heroine owns a bar. A single man has been coming into her establishment every evening at the same time for more than a year. They chat, and sometimes she sits with him for a few minutes. They flirt, but it's never gone to the next level. She decides that today is the day she's going to ask him out, but he never shows up. The next day your heroine finds a letter that her customer had written her. It says that if something happens to him she's supposed to . . .

What is she supposed to do? Does she do it, and what happened to the man?

NO. 44

Your heroine is a house flipper. She buys old derelict homes and restores them to their former beauty. The house she just purchased has many secrets. There are notes in the wall and clues under the floorboards. It's like someone is leading her to solve a puzzle.

What is the puzzle, and who is your hero? A detective? Her brother's friend? A contractor? The original owner of the home?

NO. 45

Your heroine is a caterer at a party when the venue is put on lockdown. Armed men have entered the building, and no one is supposed to leave. The event triggers a memory, and she starts having a panic attack.

What is the memory? Who calms her down, and how do they get out of the situation?

NO. 46

He thought he was meeting a man—a man named Lou. He wasn't prepared for Louisa. Now the entire plan has to be changed, and he has no idea how to hide a woman, let alone a woman who looks like her.

What are they doing, and why does he have to hide the fact that she's a woman? What happens?

No. 47

Your heroine lives alone in the wilderness, far away from civilization. An airplane crashes on her land.

Who is the pilot? Why did it crash? What does she do to save him?

NO. 48

Your heroine is a tour guide. She's leading a bus full of tourists when the unthinkable happens. She takes her job and her responsibility for the tourists very seriously and won't forgive herself if anyone dies on her watch. Your hero is on the bus and teams up with her to make sure they all survive.

What happened? Who is your hero? How does he help? Where are they?

NO. 49

Your heroine finds an antique necklace. She enlists the help of a friend to track down the family history and uncovers a series of murders are attached to the piece. Her digging also captures the attention of the murderer. He may be too old to take care of her himself, but he can hire someone to kill the nosy woman and her friend.

What happens? Who does she meet along the way that becomes her romantic interest and perhaps the person who saves her life?

NO. 50

Your heroine grew up in a military family and vowed to never get involved with a military man. When one shows up on her front porch, she may not have a choice.

Why? Who is he, and why is he at her doorstep?

NO. 51

Your heroine is mistakenly kidnapped. She's in the wrong place at the wrong time. When your hero realizes he's kidnapped the wrong woman, he decides he doesn't want to let her go.

Why did he kidnap her? Who did he mean to nab, and why? What happens?

NO. 52

Your hero's time is up. Your heroine vowed to wait for him, but she's lost hope and believes that he must be dead. She takes the painful steps of moving on without him, but he's not really dead.

What happens when she learns that he's alive? How is the situation complicated?

NO. 53

Your heroine hears a gentleman speaking Russian on the telephone. It sounds like he's in some trouble, and she offers her help in fluent Russian. He is startled that she speaks Russian and graciously accepts her help. He asks her to deliver a duffel bag to someone. He even opens the bag to show her that there's nothing illegal inside. But there is, and when she hands the bag over to the right person all heck breaks loose.

Who is he, and what's inside the bag?

NO. 54

Your heroine isn't adapting well to her new job in rural Wyoming. She loves the ranch house she's renting, and her landlord is pretty spectacular to look at, but the coyotes and the cowboys seem dangerous. Small town life isn't what it's cracked up to be, especially when a dead body shows up on her back porch. Together she and her dangerously sexy landlord try to figure out what happened.

Who died, and how did they die? What is her new job and the reason she had to move to Wyoming?

No. 55

Your heroine's best friend and sorority sister from college is brutally murdered. At the funeral, another sorority sister is killed. One by one they're being targeted.

Why? What happened in college that angered your villain? Who is your hero, and how does your heroine meet him?

EROTIC

Eroticism, Ménage, BDSM

Your heroine is traveling on her own when she finds herself in a sticky situation. She meets two men who offer to help her out in exchange for . . .

What are their conditions, and what sticky situation is your heroine in? How does she respond to their offer?

NO. 57

Your heroine is the editor of a popular entertainment blog at a magazine. When her review of a sexy, scandalous new book is scathing, the author comes knocking at her door. She can't deny her immediate attraction and feels badly for her review—maybe she was a bit harsh. To make it up to him, she offers to take him out to dinner to discuss how she might make amends. He counters with a different sort of proposal.

What does he offer? Does she take him up on it?

NO. 58

It is Friday night. Your heroine is starting a new job, a dream job, on Monday, and to celebrate, she is going out on the town with the girls. She meets a guy, and they have a hot, intense, and spectacular night. She walks into her office Monday morning, is introduced around to the team, and guess who her boss's boss is?

How does he respond? How does she?

Your heroine has a normal day job as an accountant, but also a secret life a dominatrix. She has never let anyone dominate her until she meets a new client.

What happens between them that changes her life forever?

NO. 60

Your heroine is a bartender for hire. She works private parties for wealthy people who can afford to hire a private bartender. She's seen a lot but she's not prepared for tonight's festivities.

Who is hosting the party? What does she witness, and what is she invited to participate in? How does she respond?

NO.
61

Your heroine is an artist. When she hits a creative block she uses sex to recharge. She just found a conquest but instead of fueling her, he drains her. Now she can't paint anything. Why? How does she fix it? (Maybe she learns that casual encounters no longer work and she has to find someone she loves to recharge her creative energy.)

NO. 62

Your heroine is a sexual matchmaker. She gets paid big bucks to read people and match them to their perfect physical mate. Until today she's never met hers. Now he's right in front of her.

What happens?

NO. 63

Your hero is wealthy and can have anyone and any experience he desires. He's not prepared for your heroine. He wants her like he's never wanted anything or anyone before, but she's making him jump through one ridiculous hoop after another. It's well worth the wait, and now he's just not sure what to do when he can't get enough of her.

What is so compelling about your heroine, and why does she make him jump through so many hoops?

Your hero has been watching over your heroine for years. He's stayed back behind the scenes and used his influence to eventually get her to work for his company. Now that she's right in front of him every day, he's struggling to keep his cool.

What happens when she finds he's been manipulating her for years? What does she ask from him to help make amends?

NO. 65

Your hero's kid sister's best friend is all grown up, but she's still frightfully awkward and in need of some help. When she comes to him for "experience" and a sexual education he's surprised that she's able to teach him a few things about life and love.

What happens between them?

NO. 66

Your heroine is a party planner and specializes in helping rich men spend their money extravagantly. She has one strict rule; don't date the clients. But when her party for your hero turns into a fiasco leaving them stranded, they make the most of it.

Where and how are they stranded? What happens that makes them stranded? (For example, maybe they host the party on a small island and a hurricane warning causes them to evacuate, but they're both too busy making sure everyone else is cared for that they get left behind.)

NO. 67

Your heroine loves matchmaking, but her latest targets just aren't cooperating. In fact, they both seem more interested in her than in each other.

What happens? Why does your heroine enjoy matchmaking more than she enjoys pursuing her own love life? How do her targets convince her otherwise, and who wins her heart—one of them or both?

HISTORICAL

Regency/Victorian,
Celtic, Pirate

NO. 68

Your heroine is trapped. She's been captured by someone and is being held against her will.

Who captured her? Why did they capture her? For example, is she a spy, or is her captor an obsessed person? How long has she been held? What is her plan to escape? How does she get out? Does anyone help her escape? What is the first thing she does when she gets free? How does her captor respond? Does he or she hunt your heroine down? Do they go after someone she loves? What happens?

NO. 69

Your heroine is pregnant, and to protect her unborn baby, she must flee. She gives birth. Life on her own is difficult, and she must be wary of all strangers. Anyone at any time may come to take her child. She finds a protector in your hero but struggles to trust him.

How do they meet? Why must she protect her child? Why do people want it dead? Describe the first time your hero and heroine meet.

NO. 70

Your hero's brother died at the hands of his betrothed's father. She feels responsible for her fiancé's death even though it wasn't her fault. Your hero comforts her but is then called off to war. When he returns many years later, he discovers that she hasn't really ever gotten over the guilt of his brother's death. She's hardened. He tries to break through the walls she's built up. How does he get through? What happens?

NO. 71

Your heroine is on a ship that's attacked by pirates. The ship's officers successfully capture the pirates' dashing captain. Your heroine realizes that she may have a good use for him. Later it turns out that your hero, the pirate captain, allowed himself to be captured.

Why? What is his goal? Who is your heroine, and what is her plan?

NO. 72

Your once-shamed hero has returned home to clear his name and to marry a woman of wealth and stature. The woman he's set his sights on is anything but the vulnerable socialite he believed her to be, and he is unaware that she holds the secret to clearing his name. Also unbeknownst to him is the fact her fortune is vastly overrated.

What happens between them?

NO. 73

Your heroine leaves home to avoid having to marry a man she hates. She volunteers as a nurse during the war. She develops a relationship with a soldier but is called back home when her father is murdered.

What is the connection between the soldier she's grown to love and her father's murderer?

Your heroine sells herself to the highest bidder to escape her father's brutal reign. Who buys her? Why? And what happens to threaten the life they begin to build together?

Your heroine is determined to clear her father's name. As she uncovers his secrets . . .

What did her father do? Why is she compelled to clear his name? Who is your hero, and how does he help or hinder your heroine on her quest?

NO. 76

Your hero is tired of being chased for his status and fortune. He takes off one night and finds himself at the mercy of a woman who threatens to end his life.

Who is she? Why is she so guarded against your hero and so capable of protecting herself? How does he convince her that he's no threat while still keeping his identity a secret?

NO. 77

Your heroine was just humiliated. She's standing alone, and all eyes are on her. Your hero steps in to "rescue" her.

What happened to her, and why was she intentionally humiliated? Why does your hero step in to rescue her? Who is he, and what does he do to save the day? How does your heroine thank him, or does she? Maybe she's too embarrassed and runs off. If so, how does he find her?

Your heroine, married to a Scottish king, must produce an heir in order to take her rightful place in her kingdom. Unfortunately, the royal healer tells her that her husband isn't capable of passing down his family's genes, but his brother is.

What does she do? What happens?

NO. 79

Your heroine visits a seer and is told that her father is dying. The person tells her that her father will not be giving the crown to her when he dies, but rather he will confer it upon someone else.

Is the seer telling the truth? If not, why not? If he or she is, then who does her dying father give the crown to, and how does your heroine react? Who is your hero? For example, is your hero the man who is offered the throne? Does she like him or despise him at first?

No. 80

Your heroine is a historian who collects ancient Celtic tapestries. One tapestry captivates her, and when she finally acquires it, she's zipped back in time and finds herself at the mercy of a madman. A Celtic warrior comes to her aid.

Why? Why does the madman have your heroine, and how does she react when she realizes she's traveled back in time? Does she stay, or does she, and her warrior, find their way back to the present?

INSPIRATIONAL

Christian,
Spiritual, Forgiveness,
Moral Themes

Your heroine is an attorney in a class-action lawsuit. She realizes, a little too late, that she is on the wrong side. The owner of the company is not only insanely attractive but he's also kind, honest, and he has integrity—unlike the people suing him.

What does she do? How do they get together? What is the class-action lawsuit about?

NO. 82

Your heroine just received custody of her deceased sister's young child. Now she must discover the identity of the child's father. Your heroine feels it's important for the child and the right thing to do.

What happens when she learns who the father is? Is it someone she knows? How does she find him? What happens between the two of them, and how do they fall in love?

Your heroine lost her husband/fiancé in a tragic airplane accident. On the anniversary of his death, she returns to the isolated place of the accident. She sees someone in the distance and believes it to be her dead husband/fiancé.

What happens? Is it him or someone that looks like him? Does he run away or stick around to explain what he's doing there? If it is her dead husband/fiancé, why is she seeing him now?

NO. 84

Your heroine makes hats for children and into each hat she weaves a heavenly wish—one that she knows will come true.

What does she do when she meets a very special child? How does her wish affect the child's single father? What happens when the child's wish is granted? What is the wish, and why is the child special?

NO. 85

Your heroine takes an online genetics test and not only discovers that her parents aren't her real parents—she's adopted—but also that current boyfriend is related to her. It's a good thing they haven't had sex yet. The genetics test also connects her with her biological family.

What happens when she tries to break it off with her boyfriend? What does she do about her newly discovered family? Who does she meet? What does she learn about herself?

Your heroine dies. While she is on the other side, she sees/experiences something that makes her fight to come back. She wins the fight.

What does she see, and what happens when she comes back?

Your heroine has a strong faith and an impenetrable moral code. A famous musician's tour bus breaks down in front of her home. Face to face with the "bad boy" of country music/rock music, she cannot turn him down when he and his driver are in need. She agrees to put him up in her large farmhouse while the bus is repaired. Little does she know that the musician, whom she's extremely attracted to, is tired of his life and looking for meaning and a purpose. When he meets your heroine a little of his faith is restored—after all, it's not every day that you meet an angel.

How does your hero convince your skeptical heroine that he's a changed man?

NO. 88

Your heroine runs a teen group home where she helps troubled youth. Tragedy strikes, and vandals destroy the safe haven she's worked so hard to build. She begins questioning her faith and her purpose.

How does she find her way back? Who is your hero? What does your hero do, and how does he help her? What originally happens to her group home that brings the two of them together?

Your heroine is a home caregiver. The grandson of the woman she's caring for comes barging into the home one day. He's upset.

What is he upset about, and how does your heroine handle the confrontation? (Maybe the grandmother did something to intentionally draw him to the home—she's playing matchmaker.)

NO. 90

Your heroine is in a coma. She can hear what's going on around her but cannot respond to it. To pass the time, she begins to create stories in her head. All the scenarios she imagines star the same man. He talks to her, and they develop a relationship.

What happens when she wakes from her coma, and she comes face to face with him for the first time?

YOUNG ADULT

ADULT

First Love,
Teen Supernatural

NO. 91

Your young hero lives by himself deep in the woods. A forest fire forces him out of his home. On the run from the flames, he comes across a girl.

Why is she in the woods? Why does your hero live alone in the woods? How do they escape the fire? What happens when they meet, and how do they meet?

Your hero witnesses two men harassing a woman and her teenage daughter in a parking lot.
What does he do? What happens?

No. 93

Your heroine is searching for her long-lost brother. She believed him to be dead, but recent clues indicate that he is still alive. Is he still alive? Who helps her through this process? Is he an old friend for whom she develops feelings? Is he someone new that she meets? (Maybe he's the son of a police officer, and she thinks he can convince his dad to help her. He helps her instead, and they fall in love.)

No. 94

Your young and quite spunky heroine is dumped because her boyfriend learns that her great-grandmother was a witch. Feeling hurt and betrayed, your heroine breaks the rules and uses her powers to get revenge on him. Her actions bring down the wrath of her family, her boyfriend's family, and the witch's council.

What happens? Who comes to her aid and helps her get out of this mess? How does she get her revenge?

NO. 95

Your heroine is a young fairy with the powers of seduction. She's just coming into her powers, and the desire to use them is becoming overwhelming. She has one boy in her sights, and she's just not sure what to do. Her mother is gone, and she has no one around that she can turn to.

How does she navigate the new powers and desires? Who helps her? What mistakes does she make?

NO. 96

Your heroine's best friend is a boy; they've been friends since birth and have grown up together. This summer is going to be their first summer apart.

What happens? Where is she going? Does he follow her? Does he get a girlfriend? Does she meet someone new?

Your heroine is out with friends. They're invited to a party by a group of boys they just met. Things quickly get out of hand at the party. A young man comes to your heroine's rescue. They leave the party, and she finds herself feeling safe and free as they wander the streets of the city together.

Who is he? What happens at the party? What adventures do they have that night, and what happens when the sun comes up?

NO. 98

Your heroine has always had some pretty vivid dreams. They started when she was a child, but now they're getting out of control . . . and they're always starring the same person (or people).

What does she do when she realizes that they're not dreams at all? What are they if they're not dreams? For example, are they memories, or does she travel to another place? Who is the person (or people) she's dreaming about? What happens?

No. 99

Your heroine's friends decide its time she has a boyfriend, and they create a plan to help her find one. They create a formula based on a boy's answers to a few key questions.

What happens when your heroine's best friend's brother—whom she's had a crush on for years—fits the bill better than any of the others?

NO. 100

Your heroine attends a private school with dark secrets. As she stumbles onto one of the secrets, someone is determined to shut her up. Her two best friends, who are both deeply in love with her, try to protect her and solve the mystery before it's too late.

What's the secret your heroine stumbles on? What happens, and who is trying to keep her quiet?

MY PLOT IDEAS

_____
_____
_____
_____
_____
_____
_____
_____
_____
_____
_____
_____
_____
_____
_____
_____
_____
_____

_____

_____

_____

_____

_____

_____

_____

_____

_____

_____

_____

_____

_____

_____

_____

_____

_____

_____

_____

_____

_____

_____

MY PLOT IDEAS

ABOUT THE AUTHOR

Annette Elton is the author and ghostwriter of more than 25 books. She's been a professional book reviewer for a national magazine and is currently a writing confidence and creativity coach. Annette is also the author of *1001 Romance Story Starters: Writing Prompts to Spark Your Imagination*, as well as three paranormal romance novels published under the name Annette Brownlee.